I0102340

The #Know #Like #Trust Expeditor:

How to Ignite Your Sales with Social Media

Kindle Direct Publishing a ™ of Amazon.com Inc.

P.O. Box 81226

Seattle, WA 98108-1226

kdp.amazon.com

866-321-8851

©2020 Tristen Sutton Consulting, LLC. All Rights Reserved.

No part of this book may be reproduced, stored in a retrieval system, or transmitted by any means without the written permission of the author.

ISBN: 978-1-7350340-0-3

Dedication

To my wife, CC Sutton, who has been my biggest supporter and my constant motivator… I would not be the man I am today if you were not in my life. Thank you for being my everything because without you I am nothing.

Contents

Acknowledgements

Thank you to my editorial team, Krystal Berry, Joy Diggs, and CC Sutton. Without their help, this book would be full of typos and grammatical errors. They are the real MVP's by helping me get this book organized in a format that you will enjoy reading.

Chapter 1:

#Welcome to My Page

You can buy attention (advertising). You can beg for attention from the media (PR). You can bug people one at a time to get attention (sales). Or you can earn attention by creating something interesting and valuable and then publishing it online for free (social media).

-David Meerman Scott

Picture It. January 2020. You're a social media buff. You have Facebook, Instagram, Snapchat, LinkedIn, Tinder…okay, maybe we're not going that far, but you have social media platforms. And in 2020, you still don't believe that social media can enhance company brand recognition and increase business connections. Well, consider this: in a world where connections and relationships matter, social media is the ultimate tool for connecting with others. It's a conduit that provides consistent and convenient access to your brand persona on a daily basis.

Social media provides a platform for businesses to put away the business cards as first greetings and truly build deeper relationships with potential customers.

Every day, you give people a convenient chance to get to know who you are, what you like, who you spend time with, and what you stand for. If you tried this with conventional methods, it would be virtually impossible to keep up with everyone in your rolodex, phone book, or even your customer relations management system (CRM).

But with the tap of a screen, I can instantly see what's going on in the lives of the people I'm connected to on social media. And if I'm connected to the right ones, they can see the same for me. Who has time to call everyone in their phone list every day to check on them? No one. What about emailing everyone? Nope. But if we're connected on social media, I can scroll, engage, and connect with you consistently in an unobtrusive way and make more genuine connections. If I go to your timeline every other day and simply like or comment on a post, that won't seem creepy to you. Why not? Well, simply put, it's the psychology of social media.

We post with an expectation of getting a #like or a #comment. For those of us who consider algorithms, we recognize which types of posts get the most attention from our audience. If my posts are historically funny, a serious post may or may not garner the response I'm looking for. We've also figured out what time of day is best to post. For many users, there is a particular window of time that their posts can peak. For some users, this time frame doesn't matter. For those who are impacted by timing of a post, it's imperative to post during peak times.

And how could we ever forget the #emoji? Users love it more if you put an #emoji like the "LOL" or love face on a post. Even #gifs have found their footing in social media. Whereas emojis give us a still version of reactions to posts, #gifs provide a more interactive response.

Now, on the other hand, if we're not that well acquainted and I call, text, or email you every day, that would seem very weird, right? But the truth is, social media is still a form of communication and engagement, just like the latter. What makes the one with more frequency less intrusive than the latter options? #Psychology. It's just that simple. You're conditioned to seeing random people online engaging with your posts. You downright expect it if we're being honest!

Sometimes, we actually encourage it by asking people to "comment below" or, the infamous, "like or share this post."

So why is this important to relationship building within your business?

Traditional methods of connecting and rapport building can take hours, weeks, or months, but social media virtually allows this to happen instantaneously. By strategically showcasing, to the world, who you are, you allow people to decide if they #Know, #Like, or #Trust you based on what you present, and quicker than traditional methods. Perhaps it's because they identified with something you posted. Perhaps they were inspired by something you posted. Perhaps they were even influenced by the #Trust of those on your friends list or the random comments and likes to your posts overall. Social media is one of the quickest ways to connect you to the people who are seeking what you have to offer. By providing consistent and convenient access to your brand persona, your potential customers can #Know, #Like, and #Trust you before you even meet.

#Like. #Comment. #Subscribe.

Have you ever noticed this phrase under a link, video, photo, or post of someone who is attempting to engage or keep their audience? It is relationship building for Social Media 101. A vital part of developing a **#Know #Like #Trust** factor with your followers, who may potentially patronize your business, is to cultivate a relationship with them. You cultivate that relationship with them by inviting them to *take action*.

So, at the end of each chapter, that's exactly what I'm inviting you to do. *Take action!* If you are serious about implementing this model for your business, it's time to have a plan that can boost engagement with your business.

Take the time to **#Like #Comment #Subscribe**.

Based on the topic of each chapter, complete the following actions items:

#**Like-** What key point(s) can you take away from this chapter that will enhance business likeability?

#**Comment-** Based on what you #**like**, how can you use that to express brand personality to increase business likeability?

#**Subscribe-** Create a plan of action to accomplish this.

#Like. #Comment. #Subscribe.		
#Like	What key point(s) can you take away from this chapter that will enhance business likeability?	
#Comment	Based on what you **#like**, how can you use that to express brand personality to enhance business likeability?	
#Subscribe	Create a plan of action to accomplish this.	

<u>Chapter 2:</u>

View My #Profile

You are what you share.

-Charles Leadbeater

According to Bob Burg, contributing writer to American City Business Journals,

Unlike its stereotype, business networking is not based on hitting up every new person you meet with some line about how great your product or service is while slapping a business card into their hand and uttering clever one-liners such as, "let's do lunch." I often define networking as, "the cultivating of mutually beneficial, give and take, win/win relationships." The focus is on the "give" part.

In the world of business, our traditional forms of networking and connecting are to attend an event, exchange cards, follow up with an email, schedule a lunch or coffee meeting, meet and attempt to build rapport, leave the meeting, and pretty much not hear from that person again. It's a cycle that does not always bring to fruition the ideal networking opportunity that we originally seek. And soon, our attendance at networking events can become stalemate simply because we become so robotic in form. Ironically, social media can step in and help with this issue.

Our ability to consume so much of each other's personal persona, in a casual method, allows us to connect quicker from a psychological standpoint. This makes us feel like we can get to know someone more instantaneously versus taking weeks and months to form that same type of connection. And how exactly does this work on your **#profile**? **#Visibility.**

According to Infinity Group Consulting,

*It's about being seen; you can sell the most life-changing service in the world, but if you never tell anyone about it, then no one will ever benefit, and, the truth is, you don't really have a business if you don't have any customers. Secondly, visibility means that your brand becomes noticeable, important, or even famous. These two things go hand in hand because **visibility is about being seen by the RIGHT people, at the RIGHT time…** you have to put your offering out there in the first* *place, but then you need to market it with a message that will attract and resonate with people who actually want what it is you have to offer.*

Visibility expedites the #Know #Like #Trust factor. If you post pictures of you and your family eating at an Italian restaurant, I feel more connected to you if I enjoy Italian, as well. I will feel like I #Know more about you. I may even learn about a new spot to try, so now I feel grateful to you subconsciously. With this same post, I can see that you enjoy spending time with your family. You appear more well-rounded, and that helps me #Like you more. In addition, when you post a picture of you and a smiling client, my #Trust meter increases because of this "social proof." If they're happy, it must be good.

Essentially, social proof is the validating variable in our sales equation. People will look at Google, Yelp, and Amazon reviews before they make a purchase, but there's an additional factor that can sway them your way in the purchase process. Seeing people, they **#Know**, **#Like**, or **#Trust**, purchase your products or services, makes a huge impression on them. If I've been considering purchasing a new home and have no idea where to start looking for a realtor I can trust, what's the first thing I do? I could use Google and hope to find a profile I connect with in a sea of options.

My other alternative is to ask for recommendations from someone I know. Now, imagine you're in the same position. But before you start typing "local realtor," in the search bar, or begin texting your friend, you scroll down your newsfeed on social media and see a picture of a friend smiling next to the realtor that just sold them their new home.

Naturally, you would say to yourself, *maybe I should reach out and ask how the experience was with the realtor!* From a single picture and a little less than a 200-character post, you will gather that 1) my friend **#Knows** the realtor, 2) my friend seems to **#Like** the realtor, and 3) my friend obviously **#Trusts** the realtor.

That exact feeling is what we, in the marketing world, identify as "social proof."

You've seen someone who you have a connection with, or someone who appears similar to you, have a good experience with a service provider, and your trust level with this virtual stranger has already been established before you have even spoken to them. It's happened for me too.

During a pretty standard work week for me, I was able to meet with a client, Maria Lewis, who is an amazing real estate broker. We sat down to discuss social media advertising and strategies for her brokerage organization. Her work in the organization is quite impressive. I was most certain that great content would come from her soon after that meeting.

Following the meeting with Maria, I did as I normally would—I posted a photo of her and I to my Facebook page. I gave the post a few hashtags such as: #MondaysWithMaria, #CertifiedFaceBookAdsExpert, #MarketingStrategist, and even added a bit of comic relief with the hashtag #NewUniform since I was styling fresh kicks, a briefcase, and a fedora. Of course, the photo garnered likes and comments, but there was more to this moment.

Once users began to check out my profile, they soon noticed that I am also an insurance agent with State Farm. Since several of Maria's clients will eventually need insurance for their new property purchases, for many users, it was the ultimate convenience. No, they didn't know me, but they knew Maria, so they trusted her judgment to do business with me.

Honestly, this concept has been ingrained in our lives well before social media was invented. It's similar to hearing people say, "My dad drives a Chevy truck, so I drive a Chevy truck." Or, "My mom has always shopped at this department store, so I shop at this department store." When people we trust, or have similarities with, use social media to showcase a recent purchase, it builds a certain level of credibility for that item. It causes us to think, *if it's good enough for them, it might be good enough for me.*

Consider how many restaurants you've dined in simply because your friend checked in there or posted a picture of their food on social media. Again, you think to yourself, *if it's good enough for them, it might be good enough for me.*

Visibility allows potential clients to interact with your brand and builds your social proof. This expands to their circle of family and friends. Social proof is a strategic way to gain the trust of potential clients before you ever have a chance to introduce yourself.

	#Like. #Comment. #Subscribe.	
#Like	What key point(s) can you take away from this chapter that will enhance business likeability?	
#Comment	Based on what you **#like**, how can you use that to express brand personality to enhance business likeability?	
#Subscribe	Create a plan of action to accomplish this.	

Chapter 3:

#Know. #Like. #Trust.

All things being equal, people do business with, and refer business to, people they know, like and trust.

-Bob Burg

*So, what exactly is **#Know, #Like, #Trust** and how does it affect business?*

One of my marketing consulting clients was only getting business from word of mouth referrals and the occasional Google search lead. So, I did a personal social media account audit and discovered that she never posted about her real estate business on her personal account. When I asked her why, she stated, "I don't want to spam my friends and family." My suggestion to her was simple and in her comfort zone: *make one real estate related post, per week, on your personal account. It could be a picture of you at a home closing with a new client, one of you viewing a new property, or even at an open house you were hosting.*

The benefits of doing something like this, strategically and sparingly, is that it doesn't "spam" your audience; it reminds people of what you do and offer. Lastly, it shows social proof of you actually making sales which loosely translates that you must be somewhat good at what you do.

After implementing this strategy for three consistent weeks, she landed her first home sale from her personal Facebook account. The sale came from a friend she went to college with. Her friend had forgotten that my client was a real estate agent and she needed to sell her home quickly. This resulted in her inboxing my client after she saw her Facebook post. They scheduled a call and, four weeks later, my client sold her first home from Facebook.

Each of those posts she made, over that 3-week period, were free and took less than a minute to make. *How many deals are you missing out on by not reminding your audience of what you offer on a consistent and strategic basis?* Since they were Facebook friends, her client already **#knew** and **#liked** her. People do business with those they **#Know, #Like, and #Trust.**

This successful business practice is exactly what Bob Burg means when discussing **#know #like #trust:**

Successful selling has become more relationship-oriented; more relational than transactional. People want to do business that way, and who can blame them? After all, the trust factor between human beings (and especially as it relates to business) is probably at an all-time low. Prospects are worried about being schemed, scammed, taken advantage of, or just not treated right. They want to do business with someone they know, like and trust. That's also the type of person they are willing to refer to those they care about.

When we find strategic, yet tactful, ways to get our satisfied clients to share their purchase experience on social media, we are subliminally getting them to vouch for the quality of what we offer to hundreds, if not thousands of their followers. This is virtually free advertisement for your business!

The same applies to you and your social media accounts. When you post that same picture on your timeline, you're sharing with your audience that you actually have people that buy what you sell.

Several mental actions occur when your audience sees this:

- They're reminded of what you do.
- You're invoking the *if it's good enough for them, it might be good enough for me* thought process.
- You're building trust with your audience.
- You're solidifying what it is that you do.

● ● ● ●

#Know:

to have developed a relationship with (someone) through meeting and spending time with them; be familiar or friendly with (source: Google.)

In the world of sales, whether you're an entrepreneur or sales professional, people have a higher probability of purchasing something from you if they are aware of you and/or your brand. There are sales that occur every day simply because of relationships.

Stephanie Polluck, of Stephanie Polluck Media, says this,

I KNOW YOU: this is where it starts. This step is all about visibility. Before you can even think about selling to someone, they first need to know you exist. You need to be on their radar. Seems straightforward, but for many entrepreneurs, getting visible is one of their primary challenges.

#Knowing is the first step in the equation. People can't naturally #like or #trust you if they **#know** nothing about you. Social media allows people to "**#know**" you almost instantly. If someone scrolls down your timeline and takes a good look at your posts, they can come to their own conclusion about who you are, what you're about, and what you stand for. This is why it's important you're strategic with what and how you post on social media. If you're too controversial, you may turn some people off. If you promote your offerings too much, you may turn people off.

●●●●

#Like:

similar to; possessing the same characteristics or qualities.

Business **#likeability** is huge when it comes to social media. It was rapper 50 Cent who, in the last decade, re-coined the phrase "hate it or love it," and truthfully, it applies to social media too. Depending on what you post or who you're posting to, users will hate or love your profile.

A former Facebook executive once discussed the strategies behind the initial like button and how it evolved into the initial emoji. If you made a post and someone liked it, users had a sense of euphoria and it made them want to stay on the platform because of the emotional response they received from it.

Potential clients will **#like** and/or **#love** your business via your ability to share resonating content with them. In sharing online conversations, we can establish true connections. When we intentionally make sales more about relationships, people will start to get what I call the "warm and fuzzies." And it's because they #like you. "Warm and fuzzies" are what help people feel more connected with you and your business. And when people #know you and #like you, #trust can be inevitable.

●●●●

#Trust:

to be reliable; related to reliability and strength.

Stephanie Pollock also suggests that the following 6 C's of business will create #trust: consistency, congruency, clarity, communication, compelling, and constant. In essence, she suggests these characteristics become the foundational model for your business. They become your brand. And when people know your brand is synonymous with quality and that you stand behind your offerings, they will **#trust** you.

My first opportunity to be an expert contributor on a local news channel happened because of Facebook. A (strategic) Facebook friend was producing a morning segment related to one of the services I offered. When asked to find a subject matter expert, I was the first and only person she requested to be a guest. After I filmed the segment, viewed by millions of Houstonians, I asked my Facebook friend why she requested me, and her response blew me away. She replied,

"I've been following you on Facebook, and I see that you are well respected in this industry. You have been consistent with your brand on social media, so I felt you were the best fit for this opportunity."

This opportunity afforded me the chance to be an expert contributor three additional times and present my brand in front of millions of viewers each time. This ultimately allowed more people the opportunity to **#Know, #Like, and #Trust** me. **When you consistently and clearly communicate through social media, you not only build trust that connects you to potential**

clients, but you can also attract big opportunities to help grow your business.

.

#Like. #Comment. #Subscribe.

#Like	What key point(s) can you take away from this chapter that will enhance business likeability?	
#Comment	Based on what you **#like**, how can you use that to express brand personality to enhance business likeability?	
#Subscribe	Create a plan of action to accomplish this.	

Chapter 4:

#Timeline: How It's "Post" to Be

What happens in Vegas stays in Vegas; what happens on Twitter stays on Google forever!

-Jure Klepic

Posting on social media opens a window to who you are or how you want people to perceive you. You get to paint the picture of yourself one post at a time. Each time you put something on your social media #timeline, you're applying a paint stroke to the picture of the public's perception of you. Where else can you allow potentially thousands of people to interact with you personally, on a daily basis, in real-time?

That's the beauty of social media. Users log in everyday with the expectation of engaging with people-- not their email, not blogs, but social media. It's one of the only free platforms where you can connect with people on a broad scale each and every day.

Eighty-five percent of social media consumers access it from the comfort of their own phones, giving you access to billions of people at the tip of your fingers. On a daily basis, you have an opportunity to build relationships you may have never had a chance to in "real life." Social media gives people a peek into our lives in a format that wasn't possible before.

Ramona Emerson, contributor at Allure magazine, believes,

It's relatively easy these days to know a whole lot about strangers who have no idea who we are—and our brains tend to translate knowing into liking. Since the 1950's, social scientists have been aware that the more you see someone, the friendlier you are towards them.

So, how is my **#timeline** affected by this?

People feel like they know you because they have instant access to you. Access that once took weeks, months, or even years, can now happen with the scroll of a finger. I can already hear some of your thoughts as you read this. *Tristen, I'm a private person. I don't want people in my personal business.*

Well guess what? You're in control of what people know about you. You decide what you choose to post. If you don't want the world to know about how you burned the family dinner, don't post it. If you don't want your followers to know you just had an argument with your significant other, don't post it.

In her article, "How to Infuse 'Know,' 'Like' and 'Trust' in Your Content, writer Renae Gregoire states:

Let loose with a little color and personality. Share details of the time when an experience with a customer made you break into a big smile. Is there a running joke among your staff about those Philly pretzels you must have flown in every month? Tell your audience about it. Are you in business to make life easier for a group you care about? Share it. Does your CIO like to do headstands before lunch? Yep. Sharing a detail like that instigates knowing, too.

As I suggested before, you control the brush strokes of the picture you paint on social media. You get to choose the narrative. In a later chapter, we'll discuss a posting strategy that will provide guidance on how much and what types of posts to share.

The benefit of sharing and building online relationships is when people have a need or desire, they will reach out to you first because you have created top of mind awareness. With consistency, they will remember who you are and what you do.

Another way you can use social media to exponentially increase your KNOW factor, via your #timeline, is with Facebook ads. With this tool, you can choose the right audience with laser precision and pay to place your content in the newsfeeds on their phones, tablets, and computers.

Example: Let's say you're a title company representative who wants to make sure as many realtors as possible, in a certain zip code, know who you are. You can target them with Facebook ads based on the job titles in their profile as well as their interests. This is beneficial for you because soon, when you introduce yourself in professional and social settings, people will begin saying, *I feel like I've seen you somewhere before. Do we know one another?*

With Facebook ads, you can target specific industries and professions and make sure they see your face, brand, and offerings on a consistent basis. On average, it takes eight touches to achieve brand recognition. This is how I was able to grow two profitable businesses. I ran social media ads to certain groups of people, so when they had a need or desire, they reached out to me first.

Once you have brand recognition, people are more inclined to share you with their network. Because you have created top-of-mind awareness, when someone hears a need for your product or service, they naturally want to share you as a resource. This makes them feel like a hero and like they are winning points with you because they solved someone's problem and provided you with an opportunity. Social media makes this easy because all someone has to do is tag you in a post, and an instant opportunity has been created for you to generate more revenue for your business.

Once I became more well-known on social media, I began generating two to three qualified leads on a daily basis without having to spend any additional money on marketing or ads to do so. The right people knew me and what I offered, and they began to share me with their world.

My first paid speaking engagement came from Facebook. One of my Facebook friends, who I had only met once in person, noticed my consistent posts about being an entrepreneur. Her organization wanted a speaker to discuss the journey of entrepreneurship. I may have never received this opportunity to share my message if I hadn't been connected with the decision maker on Facebook and wasn't consistent about sharing who I am, as an entrepreneur, on social media. This is a prime example of how to use your platform to generate sales opportunities that otherwise may not have been afforded to you.

The more people who #know you, the more sales opportunities you have. The more of the RIGHT people who #know you, the more conversions you will have. The #Know #Like #Trust factor expedites this process. It gets you in front of the right people and helps build your brand to bring you more business.

#Like. #Comment. #Subscribe.

#Like	What key point(s) can you take away from this chapter that will enhance business likeability?	
#Comment	Based on what you **#like**, how can you use that to express brand personality to enhance business likeability?	
#Subscribe	Create a plan of action to accomplish this.	

Chapter 5:

Let's Go #Viral

Don't say anything online that you wouldn't want plastered on a billboard with your face on it.

-Erin Bury

Now that you are aware of the importance of the **#Know #Like #Trust** factor, awareness is half the battle. You now have to implement what you know. There are many times in social media life when what we post just sort of "takes off." In most cases, this is known as "going viral." I know, you're already thinking, *how can my little post go viral? It's not even my intention.* Consider what it means to go viral: your posted words, links, videos, or images get shared by a very large group of users at a quick rate. But even going viral is not always just coincidence or happenstance.

There is a system to even the best of postings and this is one of our first steps in implementing all that we have discussed so far. Viral happens when you tap into an emotion, (happy, angry, etc.). This makes people want to share. Virality is about sharing. That means you have to create content that is highly sharable and evokes some type of emotion.

We must remember that people don't log on to social media to be sold to or make purchases. Social media is their temporary escape from reality. People log on to be distracted, be curious, and to be entertained. If all your posts are only related to your business and you're always trying to sell something, your audience is going to be turned off. And in essence, they will turn you off virtually. They may start hiding you from their timeline, unfollow you so they can't see your posts, or, worst of all, unfriend you.

Most people, even the busiest of them, can make time for two posts per day. One in the morning and one in the evening. You can switch up the order to keep things fresh. Every post has to have an objective to help expedite the **#Know #Like #Trust** factor. Before you make a post, consider these variables:

- Will this help my audience get to **#KNOW** me better?
- Will this cause my audience to **#LIKE** me more?
- Will this help build more **#TRUST** with potential buyers?

There's a saying that "all things are good in moderation." Learn how to moderate your business posts. I use a simple formula that I follow daily:

1 Personal Post + 1 Business Post + Engagement = Daily #Know #Like #Trust

And here's the importance of implementing this formula for your posts:

- Engagement (liking, commenting, etc.) causes euphoria which makes people feel more connected or closer to you.
- It generates the "warm and fuzzies."
- It's a contact sport – that's why it's called SOCIAL media. Be social, interact, and engage.

Using this formula has been beneficial to me and my business and my clients and their businesses. And the truth is, having a method-to-the-madness is essential. You need to have a planned process if you are going to make this work. Just as computers use algorithms, we too must have a process.

Here's your posting checklist. Ask yourself, will this post help me:

- Expand my brand. (**#know** me)
- Help me connect. (**#like** me)
- Provide warm and fuzzies. (**#trust** me)

Sometimes there's overlap: what I post to get you to **#like** me may also cause you to **#trust** me.

Before you make any post, consider these three variables and how it will enhance your connection with people that follow you. With time and consistency, you will start establishing virtual relationships and it will feel like you've known these people for years, when in reality, some you may have never met in person. This digital relationship or connection forms over time because you've allowed people to see who you are, what you stand for and you've welcomed them into your world.

#Like. #Comment. #Subscribe.

#Like	What key point(s) can you take away from this chapter that will enhance business likeability?	
#Comment	Based on what you **#like**, how can you use that to express brand personality to enhance business likeability?	
#Subscribe	Create a plan of action to accomplish this.	

Chapter 6:

#ENGAGEMENT IS KEY

Engage rather than sell…Work as a co-creator, not a marketer.

-Tom H.C. Anderson

You've heard me say it before, and I'll say it again, social media is a "contact sport." Make contact with people and you'll enhance your connections. These are three daily routines I follow to keep my contact rate high with my followers:

- **#Engage** with all of your comments--even it's just liking.
- Wish everyone a happy birthday.
- Find at least three people you want to expedite the #Know #Like #Trust factor with and comment on one of their posts.

In his article, "8 Ways to Build Trust on Social Media," Jayson Demers suggests that engagement builds trust, and it can be done through responding to your audience:

Depending on the size and reach of your brand, it might be impossible to respond to every inquiry, but for most brands, it's an easily accomplishable feat. When a user reaches out to you on social media with a comment on one of your posts or a question about your business, it's a demonstration that they're interested in your brand. If you respond to those comments and questions, and respond in a timely manner, you're demonstrating that you hear and care about those comments.

When responding, make sure you fully address the question or comment and don't resort to a formulaic auto-response. Write each response personally if you want to establish trust with your audience.

There are a multitude of reasons why I practice these three things on a daily basis. I'll just share a select few that I believe will help you understand the importance and impact of this methodology.

#Engaging with your comments serves two purposes: it shows that you care enough to respond to people who have taken time to type out their thoughts and feelings on your post. It doesn't have to be a long response but something to acknowledge them. This touch point helps increase your **#LIKE** factor.

The next benefit is expanded reach. At the time of writing of this book, the Facebook & Instagram algorithm considers how much **#engagement** you have on a post when it looks for posts to push into other newsfeeds. If your post doesn't have a lot of initial #engagement, it gets suppressed and seen by fewer people. By having a lot of #engagement (comments, likes, shares), your post signals to the algorithm that people are enjoying this content and that it should be shown to more people. When you reply to comments in an #engaging manner, it makes people want to come back and type more. That increases your post's awareness, which increases your brand awareness.

Additionally, the more visible #engagement (likes and comments) a post has, the better the social proof. When people see a post with 100+ likes and 150+ comments, their mind says, *Wow, this must be a good post. Let me see what else they have to say.* They will then begin looking at your previous posts. If you've been posting based on the **#Know #Like #Trust** formula, when they scroll down your timeline, they'll see a lot of social proof and personal posts that will help expedite the #Know #Like #Trust factor for you.

Remember that awesome person you met at an event you went to on a Wednesday? The day following the event, begin to engage with that person's content on Facebook or Instagram in a genuine/organic manner. If they post something funny, type the ubiquitous "LOL" or post a smiley face. If they post pictures from a recent vacation, ask about their experience. If they #post a picture of their food from a recent restaurant visit, that's an opportune time to ask if they recommend that spot for a special occasion or if they enjoyed the menu.

The point is, when **#posting,** find strategic ways to connect with people on a personal level, and eventually your business opportunities will unfold. Now, start making personal connections at a higher volume with the right people without it feeling forced or weird. Social interaction on a social media platform is expected. It's the norm. Do more of it consistently and you'll start making deeper relationships on a grander scale than traditional forms of networking.

Here's another example. Facebook sends daily birthday notifications. Even with 5,000 friends on my personal profile, I average between 7-14 birthdays a day from my friend's list. It only takes a couple of minutes to get through the entire list and send each one a personal happy birthday wish. As always, there are several reasons for this. First, it's just a nice thing to do ▨. People like to feel special on their birthday and by you taking time out of your day to acknowledge them, it instantly enhances your **#LIKE** factor.

Secondly, it helps with the algorithm. The more engagement you have with someone, the more your posts will show up in their newsfeed and vice versa. Have you noticed that you have hundreds, if not thousands of friends but only see posts from the same people? That's because the engagement between your other friends isn't high enough for Facebook/Instagram to show you each other's posts. Since neither of you are interacting often, the algorithm suppresses each of your posts from your newsfeeds. That's the primary reason you are unable to see someone's posts for a while, until you start to engage with them on their timeline.

Remember, this is a contact sport. The more you #engage, the more benefits you will reap. This additional touch point of wishing them a happy birthday helps the algorithm show more of your posts to people who are on your friends list. It's going to take more than one "happy birthday" post once a year, but this is a good start. Chances are they'll see your posts and say, *Hey, I haven't seen them on social media in a while. Let me go check out their timeline.* And it's there they will see your social proof and personal posts that will hopefully get you two reacquainted.

#Like. #Comment. #Subscribe.

Let's put these tips in action. Follow the steps below to enhance your connections and expand your reach:

1. Engage with all comments on your posts from the last 3 days, even if it's just "liking" the comments.

2. Wish everyone a happy birthday when you get the daily birthday notifications.

3. Find at least three people you want to expedite the #Know #Like #Trust factor with and comment on one of their posts over the course of the next three days.

Chapter 7:

Sitting in #Traffic

On social media, we get excited if someone follows us. In real life,
we get really scared and run away.

-Unknown

Okay, don't close the book. I know anyone reading this chapter, who happens to be from or live in Houston, Los Angeles, New York City, Washington, D.C., or any other major city, almost threw their book away. But I'm not suggesting the day-to-day #traffic we sit through, in our cars, is "good." I am suggesting good #traffic does exist. Good traffic includes the views, likes, or comments you may get at a particular time of the day. Every user is different, so using statistics provided by the social media platform can show you peak times. When it comes to social media, know that your audience is looking and listening.

Steve Rayson, of BuzzSumo, believes that authority, helpfulness, and intimacy help build trust. And building trust helps to build #traffic. In his article entitled, "How to Use Social Media to Build Brand Trust" he says,

An authority is a go-to resource for everything happening in an industry. Be that go-to resource. Share helpful articles about all of the latest news and

happenings in your realm. Here are some places to find great content to share:

- *RSS blog feeds: Actively follow what your partners, competitors, and others in the industry are sharing so you can stay on top of the latest news and share your findings.*
- *Hashtags and keywords: Follow keywords and hashtags that are relevant to your industry. You'll be able to see what others are sharing that relates to those topics.*

By finding and curating content that is resonating with your audience, or your tribe, you'll be able to drive #traffic to your social media platforms, which in turn increases visits to your website and helps create more sales opportunities.

From check-ins, to pictures, to hashtags, articles, memes and more, your audience is looking and listening. When you share content that is trending, it brings more eyes to your social media platforms to view all of your content, which ignites the #Know #Like #Trust factor.

This is why it's important to have a strategy in place that ensures you are posting content with a purpose. I use my 3-point content checklist before I make a post on any social media platform:

1. Does it align with my brand?
2. Will it help people #Know #Like #Trust me?
3. Can this offend anyone?

If a piece of content doesn't clear these three checkpoints, then it doesn't get posted. I encourage you to create your own checklist to use as your "posting beacon" so that you can have an internal standard to go by when creating content. It will help you stay on brand and provide consistency for your audience.

Another way to drive #traffic is to request pictures with your happy clients after a transaction (where applicable). 1- When you post happy client pics on your timeline, request their permission to tag them so it also shows up on their timeline in case they forget to post it. This way you still get the exposure with their authorization. 2- If applicable, check into your business location when you make the post. This is an added exposure point that allows people easy access to view your business page. 3- Always incorporate your branded hashtag to help build momentum behind your movement. It also builds up your usage volume in the search index for people who want to seek you out in the future. They'll be able to see all of your past posts with the hashtag you used.

And finally, develop something YOUnique that helps you stand out from your competition. In a cosmos of copying, plagiarism, cloning, duplicating, and counterfeiting, the extra thoughts and time into creating a tag, specific to you, can be necessary and extremely helpful. When it's YOUnique, people will automatically attribute the thought or phrase with you and/or your business.

Also include your logo in or on the picture. These extra brand touches help with brand recognition in the future. There are hundreds of free apps that allow you to add your logo to a picture right on your phone. One of my favorites is Photofy.

For example: in one of my business ventures, I used a play on my last name and mashed up Sudden Impact with "Sutton Impact." Whenever I was done meeting with a client, we would take a picture by my logo and I would use the verbiage, *my client just received the #SuttonImpactExperience*. I would then list what we accomplished in the meeting and post on my timeline and business pages. Finally, I would tag the client with their permission. The next thing you know, I'm getting inbox messages and post comments saying, *I need to meet with you because I've been looking for those services.*

This is how you get social media to work for you. You create brand personality. Those were free leads that converted into sales and additional revenue for my companies. For this to work, you're going to need to apply the strategy with consistency.

#Like. #Comment. #Subscribe.

Let's put these tips in action. Follow the steps below to develop your YOUniqueness and increase #traffic to your brand:

1. Come up with three YOUnique hashtags that you can include in all of your posts to brand your business.

   _____

   _____

   _____

   _____

   _____

   _____

   _____

   _____

2. Identify your three "Posting Beacon" principles that will serve as your content guidelines before you make a social media post.

_____

_____

_____

_____

_____

_____

_____

_____

_____

_____

3. Once a week, make a post about a satisfied client and post a picture of the client with your logo on it.

_____

_____

_____

_____

_____

_____

_____

_____

Chapter 8:

Get a #Handle on It

Social media is a great place to tell the world what you're thinking before you've had a chance to think about it. – Chris Pirillo

Welp, I don't know who needs to hear this, but I am not instructing you to start using your personal profile, especially Facebook, to start promoting and selling your offerings. After all of this information and all of these suggestions, that is more than likely not the best idea. Actually, they may shut your account down.

Ultimately, I'm suggesting that you use your personal account to strategically connect with people who may potentially buy *from* you or can be a center of influence *for* you. An important part of that ability to connect is the consistency of your account names.

Your account or social media name, also known as a **#handle,** will be associated with everything you have responded to or even posted. This is why it is essential for your social media handles to be a similar as possible.

This is where I can appreciate social media even more. There are times when a potential client or customer may not be able to remember your phone number or your email. But I can guarantee you that if you introduce them to your social media platform (s), it is much easier for them to remember.

In the event you have more than one social media account, don't panic about your names. With so many accounts being created, it's almost guaranteed for the name you need to already be taken. The key to all of this is just that: consistency. Even if your #handles are not identical, they are at least parallel in nature.

Let's say you're at a networking event and have a great conversation with someone. You two really connect and you feel like a great business relationship can form. Most people don't consider sharing social media handles and instead default to just handing them a business card or even connecting with each other on LinkedIn. The challenge here is it's a slower process to initiate the **#Know #Like #Trust** factor.

Let's be honest: LinkedIn is still "stuffy" and corporate. I feel like I need a shirt and tie on every time I log in. The content and the vocabulary are very corporate and don't leave much room for more relaxed conversation.

In my opinion, LinkedIn is a great platform for building great professional relationships over time. But due to its "corporate nature," I feel like most people on it aren't their true selves. With Facebook and Instagram, on the other hand, you get to see more of the true person— that's my opinion. I've built two profitable businesses from my engagement on Facebook and Instagram alone. Each platform has its own personality, but I have to make sure my #handles are similar.

In addition to having a consistent #handle, consider adding more people to your personal profile than just your family and friends. They more than likely already have the information they need about you and have memorized it as well. You're allowed up to 5,000 friends on Facebook and an unlimited number on Instagram. Why only share your message with people who have already bought from you or probably never will? Think beyond the group you already know and reach out to network with those who don't look like you and don't work in the same industry as you—they may not even be connected to your culture.

The key is to expand your network. Expand your reach. One strategy is to go to your Facebook personal profile settings and turn on the "Follow" option. This allows people who aren't on your friends list to still be able to view your content and interact with you. Start accepting those LinkedIn connection requests, even if you haven't met them before. Start sending connection requests to people you don't know but have connections in common with and potentially mutually beneficial reasons for you two to be connected.

Growing your business using social media is completely possible and necessary. In a world of fraud, deception, and dishonesty, the #know #like #trust factor can go a long way for turning potential customers into actual consumers. Let's face it: yard signs just aren't going to be enough to cut it for business likeability. Using social media expands your brand and even generates leads for your business. And now it's time for you to not simply just be present on it, but to level up and make it work for YOU! Put in the work now so it can do just that, and you will build relationships that last you and your business a lifetime!

#Like. #Comment. #Subscribe.

Let's put these tips in action. Follow the steps below to grow your network.

1. Have a paradigm shift about using your personal profiles to make business connections. Loosen up a little bit.

   _____

   _____

   _____

   _____

   _____

   _____

   _____

2. Turn on the "Follow" option on your Facebook personal profile.

3. Connect with 5-10 new professionals on Facebook, Instagram, and/or LinkedIn this week and list them below.

_____

_____

_____

_____

_____

_____

_____

_____

<u>Logging Off</u>

With the growing reliance on social media, we no longer search for news or the products and services we wish to buy. Instead, they are being pushed to us by friends, acquaintances, and business colleagues.

— Erik Qualman, best-selling author

So, where do we go from here? Hopefully, by now, you can see how imperative the #Know #Like #Trust factor (KLT) can be for your business. It was my intent to give you as much information as possible without making you feel overwhelmed with KLT. And now that you have all of this information, and you have also had space to brainstorm and create a plan of action, what else would you need to know?

Well, I have a few final pieces of information that will recap and even challenge you to include the KLT factor in your business model. I call it the *LIKEABILITY CHECKLIST*. These are simply parting suggestions for what I think will help increase your business likeability and can be easily incorporated into your daily routine.

Be Yourself

A few years ago, I had someone, via social media, make an assertion that Suge Knight and I could be twins. Allow me to clarify-- this was solely based on looks.

Anything otherwise is not the business I am attempting to promote. But the joke was made, and I embraced it. It took off like wildfire! Family, friends, acquaintances, and colleagues alike all played along for such an uncanny resemblance between Suge and I.

So, I began using the hashtag #NetworkingWithSuge and it was a hit! I knew users would engage with the post simply because of the hashtag. But this also allowed them to laugh a little while simultaneously being privy to the networking and business interactions I had at an event or client meeting.

I see posts all of the time reminding us to "be us." I am a huge fan of this! You don't have to run your business like everyone else does and quite frankly, your humor or eccentric prowess may just be the attraction for a new client. It's the quality of someone who is professional and can still be authentic to who they are.

Be Neutral

Even as business owners, we have all created a resume at some point. Whether you worked for a company before owning yours or you needed a resume for a position related to your business, we've written and seen them. What's interesting is that all of our accomplishments make it to that resume but not our failures. None of our lows or down moments make it to the resume because we don't want people to see that. No one sees the final grade of a C- or test you failed in college; they only know that you graduated. Viewers will see that you own your own business, but no one will see the business venture that failed before the successful one.

Here's my point: unlike a resume, remain neutral in your approach to your clients and even those potential clients. As it relates to your business likeability, you can ensure a solid KLT factor with your online network by simply being transparent and not only showing the highlights. Does it mean you have to tell every detail of your life? It absolutely does not. But share the good and bad, highs and lows, successful and unsuccessful approaches to your business.

Your connections are sure to celebrate your victories and that is wonderful. But they will also appreciate your modest transparency to be neutral about your experiences.

Engage

A part of my consulting work with businesses is to teach them how to create their own Facebook and Instagram ads to help them grow their businesses. One of the many pieces of advice I share is to ensure they are aware of statistical information, given by the platform they choose to use, to gather realistic data on engagement. This information allows business owners to study trends on marketing and advertising and include real time data for something as simple as knowing peak times for posting.

And it's an amazing feeling to be tagged in a post, literally minutes after we've ended a session, and see a business owner rave about his/her experience in our training. Even their response to the training and tagging me in the post is another form of engagement. The overall effect of engagement allows business owners to create a sense of community attached to their businesses. This sense of community will definitely help the KLT factor between your business and your clients.

Be Relevant

There is no doubt that the COVID-19 crisis has put this world in a figurative headlock. Our first concern is to the lives and safety of families, friends, colleagues and just humanity in general. In a sincere concern for humanity, there are also concerns for the business world. Social media has been huge in being able to diversify communication in such a time, but it also became even more congested as a result. And many businesses find it to be a struggle to ensure their content stands out among the rest.

I took time to develop trainings called #RonaStrategySession. These moments allow me to coach business owners on differentiating their brands in a crowded market. I explain to them how social media ads can generate leads and much more. But the use of this hashtag and approach is relevant to our current situation as a nation and world. Believe it or not, your relevance during times like these, is the difference between a follow and unfollow or a friend or unfriend request.

Share

It's more than clear that marketing and branding play a role in the KLT factor for businesses. On my social media, my network can count on at least one post, per day from me, that is in some way connected to my business. Hashtags and key phrases are easily found through a general search on social media. If we type in a particular hashtag, word, or phrase, we are privy to the hundreds of thousands or the millions of times it has been used…and who it's connected to. Sharing also attaches to social media trends and can soon be found on search engines.

My connections can even count on at least one post per week that may highlight someone else's business. That KLT factor is certainly present when sharing or recommending another business. Because my connections have KLT with my company and brand, they are likely to have confidence in recommendations that could range from great restaurants to great realtors. There is nothing wrong with sharing the spotlight!

Share. Share. Share.

Use Video

For many social media users, what they read is just as important as what they watch. And for some users, they are more inclined to share a video versus a very long and worded post. Videos also help to diversify your posts. You give your connections options for retrieving valuable information.

Aside from a diversified approach to your posts, videos can also be a more personable approach to business likeability. Clients and potential clients alike have an opportunity to see your personality in the flesh. When marketing or promoting, things like tone and inflection can make a difference when it comes to KLT.

Have Balance

Balance is the key to avoiding over promotion of your page. Posting regularly is necessary to maintain your social media presence. Social media algorithms may cause your profile to "fade to black" when you don't post, and your content won't be shown as often. But there is also the side of posting too much that can leave your connections feeling--let's face it: annoyed and exhausted.

So, here's the strategy: post twice a day. You'll make one personal post and one business post per day.

You can also take time to engage your connections by liking posts or wishing them a happy birthday on behalf of your business. You can also find three friends and comment on their pages. The diversity in your balance will ensure that your connections don't experience a form of social media "burnout."

Provide Social Proof

I recently had the opportunity to be a part of a panel discussion hosted by my beloved alma mater, Texas A&M University (And for all of you Longhorn fans out there…well, you live to fight another day). It was an opportunity for me to discuss professional life after graduating. That opportunity was shared with CNN contributor, Yodit Tewolde, and my frat brother Roland Martin, creator of Roland Martin Unfiltered.

Why was this significant? Well, aside from sharing that virtual platform with two amazing business minds, it was an endorsement of my hard work attached to larger names. In a nutshell, this is a type of social proof. Having that connection can help boost marketing for your business. Of course, this is just one type of social proof, but its importance to the KLT factor of your business cannot be ignored.

Logging Off

I hope this information and these strategies have been helpful to you, as I have used these exact strategies to build my profitable brands. Connections and relationships matter, and social media is the ultimate tool for connecting with others. This book has detailed the importance of using social media to grow a **#Know #Like #Trust** factor for your business. Consistently post relevant content, be YOUnique, and engage with your audience. Follow this blueprint for your business to grow a stronger online presence, which will attract more customers, create more opportunities, and ignite more sales. Social media is one of the quickest ways to connect you to the people who are seeking what you have to offer. Now, it's time to *take action*!

Oh, by the way…if you've enjoyed this book, please leave a review for me on Amazon.com!

Tristen Sutton is a consultant for Facebook, Certified Facebook Digital Marketer, and a Facebook Marketing Partner who works with marketing professionals, organizations, and entrepreneurs wanting to learn how to increase their revenue and brand awareness by effectively using Facebook and Instagram ads. He has been hired by Facebook to consult with them on their curriculum for their Level Up Program which is a Facebook ads training workshop taught across the globe.

As the exclusive social media ads trainer for the Houston Association of Realtors (39,000 members), he specializes in teaching organizations how to expand their brand, generate leads, and increase open house attendance with his Ads YOUniversity™ training course.

Tristen knows how to remove the confusion from learning social media ads and makes it easy for his audience to learn how to master a skill that they can implement immediately after his session. He has taught more than 1,000 professionals how to use Facebook & Instagram ads to generate more leads for their marketing and sales objectives.

He has been featured in several media outlets such as Fox News, Houston Business Journal, Houston Chronicle, and CW39.

www.ingramcontent.com/pod-product-compliance
Lightning Source LLC
Chambersburg PA
CBHW032118280326
41933CB00009B/899